maar bidi

maar bidi

next generation black writing

With an introduction by Kim Scott

Edited by Elfie Shiosaki and Linda Martin

This is a Magabala Book

LEADING PUBLISHER OF ABORIGINAL AND
TORRES STRAIT ISLANDER STORYTELLERS.

CHANGING THE WORLD, ONE STORY AT A TIME.

First published 2020
Magabala Books Aboriginal Corporation, Broome, Western Australia
Website: www.magabala.com Email: sales@magabala.com

Magabala Books receives financial assistance from the Commonwealth Government through the Australia Council, its arts advisory body. The State of Western Australia has made an investment in this project through the Department of Local Government, Sport and Cultural Industries. Magabala Books would like to acknowledge the generous support of the Shire of Broome, Western Australia.

Magabala Books is Australia's only independent Aboriginal and Torres Strait Islander publishing house. Magabala Books acknowledges the Traditional Owners of the Country on which we live and work. We recognise the unbroken connection to traditional lands, waters and cultures. Through what we publish, we honour all our Elders, peoples and stories, past, present and future.

Cover designed by Jo Hunt
Cover illustration by Kamsani Bin Salleh
Typeset by Post Pre-press Group
Printed and bound by Griffin Press South Australia

ISBN 978 1 925936 42 1

A catalogue record for this book is available from the National Library of Australia

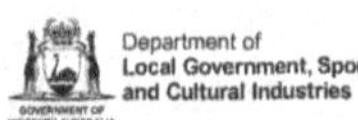

maar bidi

Tracks made by hands

We gathered on Whadjuk boodja, where Kaart Geenunginyup Bo (the place from where you can look afar) meets the beeliar, to create the stories in this collection. We acknowledge the Whadjuk people of the Noongar Nation as the Traditional Owners and honour the spirits of their ancestors and their Elders.

We acknowledge the Balladong, Bardi, Barkindji, Barrd, Bunuba, Karrajarri, Muralag, Naagufa, Nimanburr, Nunda, Nyikina, Nyul Nyul, Wagyl Kaip, Yamaji and Yawuru Countries, ancestors and Elders of the storytellers.

We thank Whadjuk Traditional Owner Len Collard for creating the Noongar language phrase maar bidi for the title of this collection. Maar bidi means to create a pathway with your hands. It could be translated as handwriting.

We acknowledge the Dean of the School of Indigenous Studies, Professor Jill Milroy, and our colleagues, for supporting this project.

Contents

Editors' note

Every year, we run a creative writing program for young Aboriginal and Torres Strait Islander students at the School of Indigenous Studies at the University of Western Australia. It is part of a pathway course that prepares students for undergraduate studies. The class sizes aren't large, usually comprising only a dozen or so students of around eighteen years of age.

In weekly creative writing workshops, the students are encouraged to find strength in their voices and write about what is meaningful to them. What it means to be young, black and passionate while encircled in divergent and often conflicting worlds. What it means to feel exuberant, enraged, confused or even unconcerned. How it feels to be on the precipice of teenhood and adulthood.

In the workshops, the students read the works of Indigenous authors along with other creative pieces from local and international writers. They look at a variety of traditional and hybrid forms. Then they shake the works down to find styles, forms and meanings that will influence their own pieces.

And in that quiet and personal space, brimming with words, ideas and influences, they create.

The stories and poems in this collection were written in these workshops. In selecting and editing we have been moved, not only by the ever-present imagination and new forms of writing, but by the heartfelt beauty and clear-eyed honesty of the writers.

The youthful voices within this collection echo The Imagination Declaration from the Youth Forum at Garma in 2019. This Declaration sounds the hope within Indigenous youth for freedom and self-determined futures.

> We don't want to be boxed.
>
> We don't want ceilings.
>
> We want freedom to be whatever a human mind can dream …
>
> We urge you to give us the freedom to write a new story (The Imagination Declaration 2019).

We hope next generations walk in the worlds dreamed up on these pages.

Elfie Shiosaki and Linda Martin

Introduction

You've picked up this book.

What to expect of an anthology with the title *maar bidi: next generation black writing*? The first two words of the title may be a little unsettling, since such marks on the page represent an endangered and ancient language rarely – at least until very recently – seen in print: Noongar.

The title *maar bidi* says hand; sinew, energy, path. Then we have *next generation black writing*.

This anthology is attempting to connect the old and the new, the ancient and contemporary. The title suggests that writing – print culture – is a way to achieve this.

We learn to make patterns of print, and despite the propensity of print to temporarily isolate its practitioners, we nevertheless use those patterns to collaborate in developing an interior space in which reader and writer meet and make meaning. What might the patterns of a book like this offer? Snapshots of people, places, perception. Young adults making sense of their world. Personal experiences, along with demonstrations of print used creatively to reveal the unique, the eternal, the new.

This anthology is made up of pieces by a diverse group of young Aboriginal and Torres Strait Islander people and thus each suggests, even if indirectly, an abiding heritage and community. As one of the editors, Elfie Shiosaki, says:

> Each writer is telling an individual story but if you map them, they are telling a story of young black Australia – and that makes it profound – because unlike other writers, Indigenous writers speak of country and kin. What does it mean for us when young Indigenous people find their voice in writing?

It is intimate, dealing with print in this way; writers craft words to gift to just one reader at a time, self to self. Read on, and you will be both recipient and collaborator.

You may wish to concentrate on these works as specific and distinctive in terms of image, event, or sensibility. You may wish to read them with context held at bay. You may prefer to consider them collectively and as somehow representative. Either way, you can expect the privilege of sharing the results of distinct individuals writing to navigate contemporary issues such as identity politics, social media and climate change. You will assist in recovering and forge a connection between an internal heritage and the external world as it is right now. You will help give voice to dreams and desires and wounds, and realise that individuals writing – and reading – can reveal and renew spirit and energy that connects us all.

Kim Scott

watchful eye of mother

Walking amongst the trees

Nancy Murray

Walking amongst the trees, I am content.

There are a million things to say, yet I am not compelled to say them.
Nature has struck wonder into my eyes, silenced my mind and filled my heart.
The temporary assortment of colours I see right now is the stuff of my dreams.
The science of our eyes is that they play tricks on us – the light controls everything we view.
Birds flit past me in a hurry. I wish them a safe flight.
Colours of tangerine, taffy and electric blue frazzle my visual,
Wafts of coconut, citrus, dairy with floral hints.
Yesterday's pressure, translates into today's rush of steam.
Breathe in,
Then out.

If I could stay here forever I would.

Its own kind of music

Angelica Augustine

The wind carries the smell of the sea to my face
the beach sand sticks to my skin
the waves get rougher

I admire the beautiful sunset
and watch the sun as it descends down
touching the rough waves
like the ocean is playing its own kind of music

Loss of innocence

Mabel Gibson

i am 8 years old. i lay with my head on my mother's lap while we swing on the love seat in the front of our property. the day is February 13 in the year 2008, it is around 10 in the morning. it is a Wednesday and although i have been up for hours i'm not going to school. i look up at the sky, so blue, i look into my mother's eyes, it's almost like i am still looking into the sky. same colour. same aliveness. surrounding our front porch are endless trees, my siblings and i spend hours exploring our own private jungle. we have so much freedom. we are so lucky. i grab my mum's hand and trace over the wrinkles with my finger. 'Mum, why am i not at school today?' i am so innocent, i know nothing of the hardships my people before me faced, i know nothing of the opportunities my people created for me through years of suffering and trauma. 'remember this morning, we watched Kevin make a speech?' i think back to 9 am, never in my life had i seen a tear roll down my dad's cheek and although i don't know what heartbreak feels like, it broke my heart watching my dad cry, were they tears of sadness or joy? 'yes, i remember, Mum, it was only an hour ago,' i giggle. 'well, when Pop was only a year older than you he was stolen from his parents.' i do not know what that means, the concept of being stolen from your own family seems unreal, even at 8 years old i know how wrong it is. 'Kevin was saying sorry for taking him away.' i look back up at the sky, so blue, but not the same as before. it will never be the same as before.

Nature

Nancy Murray

The seasons change.
Nature shifts based on her mood.

The river flows with gentle noise
There are many things carried along the surface
Lightly placed onto.

Motions in all the right ways
Wistful and ever-changing, oh so
Many connections upstream and joined
Colliding at the bottom.

Broken twigs, dead leaves, fallen branches, clouds of dirt

Swirling in sync, under the watchful eye of Mother.

Nanna's garden

Mabel Gibson

When I was younger I had an electric imagination. My mind was full of colour and so was my nan's garden. Nan often told me that I was off with the fairies, which was true. I spent hours dancing through my nan's garden with beautiful women who had opal wings that reflected electric purple when they caught the light. They had thick long hair that wrapped like blankets around their petite bodies, the strands on the ends reaching their violet glittering tutus. My nan spent a lot of time in that piece of heaven that lived at the back of her 70s-style home. My siblings and I would run through sprinklers after eating icy poles in our aunties' old t-shirts and we'd tackle each other down onto the greenest, fullest patch of grass I have ever seen. The garden was the place I would first feel the sharp sting of a tiny creature trying to protect itself from my foot. The bee that had made itself at home amongst the blossoming roses all of which resembled colours of a lover's lipstick collection. I think of how my mother would sunbathe where I danced with fairies or wrestled my siblings or screamed at the stinging sensation the bee gave me. I think of how my mum and I both at one stage of our lives picked a flower from the same soil and asked the flower if he loved us or loved us not.

When I drove past the house today I saw that they had torn down that charismatic 70s-style home and replaced it with a modern-day unit. The entire street now had the exact same house, the only difference being the numbers on each letterbox. Gone was the frangipani tree that my siblings and I would climb like monkeys while we waited for Mr Whippy's pastel pink van to show up. I remembered how we would go to the nursery and I would walk amongst the beautiful flowers and question why my nan would buy the ones that were dull and had not yet bloomed but then watch my nan take care of these dull plants for years after until they were so vibrant that the ones in the nursery could no longer compare. My nan had a way of appreciating the beautiful things before they were beautiful. I imagine that garden now. I imagine some modern couple hiring a man to spill concrete over years of history, over my nan's heart and soul. I imagine the tree that I used to pick lemons off getting murdered and being pulled out from its roots. I imagine the fairies' long faces because they can no longer dance through the roses and get their hair tangled in the stems. I know that magic cannot last forever but I do hope that my nan's magic lasts long enough for a flower to grow between the cracks in this new concrete jungle.

Nan

Nancy Murray

The beckoning of the trees, hear the urgent whispering
I think you know what awaits, your Ancestors are beckoning.
I'm sitting by the fire, johnnycakes and rabbit cooking.
Nan notices me, she sits up straight.
'What're you listening for?'
I nuzzle up to Nan. She reckons
'Sit down. Behave. I've got something to tell you.'
Strong, black woman.
Hear her as she lifts Her voice.
An endlessness of black hands raise old girl up!
I feel presence ... familiar as a hug
I listen to Her.
Wait 'til she's finished.
As she speaks, Her voice shimmers ... star-like
'My brothers and sisters were silenced for some time,
So it hurts sometimes to remember these things,
But one thing I know for sure,

Shimmering with the waters of our lands, and the ancient stories
they possess.
There are different names for Creation from all 'round,' she says.
'But you gotta listen to what our mob calls it. What we have known
it to be forever and ever.
We reckon it as *Barka*.
It branches out far and wide across far and wide,
Across different nations and our mob alike.
Every time you feel lost, just come back home to the river here,
to your kin.
Back to the *Barka*.'

My blood runs through

Savannah Cox

Home

They say home is a place where you feel most comfortable.
A place you know inside and out.
A place where no matter where you go you will always be drawn back.
It is a place where you have this special connection to where memories are made that will forever be with you. Good and bad.
For me this place is a little tourism town called Broome. To me it is more than just a place of expensive pearls and pretty beaches.
Broome is me.
My body is the land. It is solid and curved. Imperfect by man's doing but it is still beautiful and radiant.
The sky is my skin, different variations of colour represent my mixed heritage of various nationalities.
The creeks are my hair. Flowing from my body into the bay, cleansed as water flows in and out.
The red that courses through the land and stains every bit of white is my blood. My blood runs through this land as it did for my elders before me. No matter how hard you wash, it will never fade away.
Sunrises are my eyes opening wide and bright to a different day and closing when the sun sets.
The sandy dunes are my lips, softly kissed by the ocean waves and whispered to by the coastal breeze.
This is my home. It is me.

Family

They say family is the people you are related to.
Though family does not always share biological blood.
It's the connections you make with people that make them family.
My family is a tree. A big and strong tree.
All branched out in different pathways and lifestyles but connected at the roots.
I am one of many, just a small twig on a branch alongside my family members.
The leaves we produce tell our stories, our future and our past.
And when our time is up we will wither and fall.
We fall and let the wind take us.
However, our memories will forever be embedded within this big tree.
With my family I will never be alone or forgotten.
For that is how my family has always been.

Love

They say love can overcome almost anything in life.
Love is an indescribable feeling towards someone or something.
Passion, hope and perseverance.
It can get you through heart-breaking pain, worst fears and agonising sorrow.
If you can love, you can feel. If you can feel, you can love.
Love can come in all forms.
A love from a mother to a child is protection. It is eternal, with a strength so deep it will withstand time.
A love from a lover is like the ocean. Constant currents of emotions that flow both good and bad. There will be rough stormy nights that seem endless, but spray a little love and you have a calm and beautiful paradise, an infinite turquoise-blue ocean.

Love that is shared between families is endless. A love for a brother, a grandmother, an uncle, a sister. It is love you have forever.

Love for a friend is like picking a flower. You come across many but then one catches your eye and you are urged to pick it. Then you bloom together into something wonderful.

Love endures all. Always and forever no matter what form it may come.

Navigating home

Serena-May Brown

When will I be able to learn?
How can I be who I'm really meant to be
when a part of me
  feels unseen

Why didn't you teach me?
I feel lost
not knowing my history
  I'm tired of it being this mystery

When will I be able to learn?
I'm weary of waiting
I'm told by others to be the best version of myself
  but how can I, when I don't know my full self

I hear those Island drums calling
telling me to come home
reminding me that
  I'm not alone

I always have a place to go.

Take

Angelica Augustine

We have no rights,
We have no land.
That's what they say,
That's how it's planned.
Some live in fear of the white man,
But he isn't that scary.

He walks the country where our ancestors are buried.
Now tell me is that respect, is that how we should be treated?
To turn away, drop everything and leave it?
No, we are the traditional owners through and through,
Our land should be protected for me and for you.
Culture is our life and most of it is being forgotten
Like a fruit left in the sun for days, rotten.

Are you going to help us in any way or are we not worth your time?
Am I just wasting my time writing these rhymes?
So tell me, boss, what's your plan, what's your mission?
Can we count on you, Scott Morrison?
Or are you just another fake?
Say you want what's best for us but all you really want to do is *take.*

Feelings

Brianne Yarran

Dorothy Bagshaw was heading back to Carollup Native Settlement for the first time in fifty years. The four-hour drive along endless unsealed dirt roads and unforgettable memories brought back feelings she hadn't felt in a long time. Travelling back in time to a place of hurt and pain. Driving was her daughter, Sherrilyn, and in the back were her two eldest sisters, Edith and Norma, and her granddaughter, Brianne. As the roads towards the mission became more unstable so did Dorothy.

It was on the morning of 17 December 1946 that Dot and her two sisters were taken. Dot was with her mother, Violet, as Edith and Norma played by the campfire. It was a normal day, the south-western breeze spread across the red dirt. The children played along the river and the Aboriginal reserve of White Dam was mingled with joy and kindness, until a black truck pulled onto the reserve. Everyone grabbed their kids, pulling them in tight and running for shelter. The Native Welfare had determined that Violet Smith and her children would be taken.

'I don't know why Mum was taken, maybe it was because I was only a baby and Mum was still breastfeeding me.'

Two men jumped out from the truck and ran toward Edith and Norma. The girls screamed and ran for their mother, only to be grasped around the mouth and taken by the men and chucked in the back of the truck.

Flashbacks of the mission replayed in Dot's mind like temporary blind spots from the sun. One distinct memory stuck with Dot. She remembered *a red house, more like a shed*. Her sisters had no idea what she was talking about. Norma, too mentally disabled from the trauma to remember anything, and Edith, not recalling this red house from the mission. As the family pulled into the driveway of Carollup, silence and heaviness filled the car. The eyes of the sisters wandered as they were taken back to the time when they were last brought here. Except this time they were without their mother. They hopped out of the car and walked among the memories left by over 200 children.

Edith led the way, showing the family where they'd slept, eaten and gone to school, but still the red house was nowhere in sight. All of a sudden, Dot started wandering around like a lost child searching for the unknown. Her feet and the gravel had met once again, but this time with more weight and age. Her hands brushed the bushes, where her mum had comforted her many years ago. She weaved and turned not realising what she was doing. Her sisters watched with confusion and curiosity. Dot disappeared behind some unkempt bushes that covered an old, almost unrecognisable structure. The rest of the family followed but left distance, trying not to disturb the spirits that guided Dot. Her sisters watched in awe as Dot pulled back the bushes, revealing the red house. Edith remembered. *The jail*, she whispered.

A dream

Angelica Augustine

I have a dream
a dream dreamt by my mother before me
and my grandmother before her.
A dream that the land of our ancestors,
our sacred land, remains untouched.
That the natural beauty of this country
is not destroyed by greedy mining companies
stuffing their pockets with filthy money
made by exploiting the land on which I was raised.
A dream that the roads we take to
access our country are not damaged by tourists
with their flash boats and large caravans
that enter disrespectfully onto my country
without permission.
A dream that my nieces and nephews can grow
and live off this land as I have;
that the knowledge learnt is cemented in their hearts
and is practised on the grounds
where my grandparents are buried.

Mother Earth

Savannah Cox

You say mining is for a better future
But what future will be better if all land is mined?
Every hole you carve from her
She dies a little.

You say it's beneficial for people
But how does it benefit our mother we call Earth?
Pipelines draining gallons and gallons of her lifeblood
She dies a little.

Sucking out the soul of her every day
Into the pockets of people with
Ambitions only to have power and wealth,
She dies a little.

I have a dream

Nancy Murray

Dreaming is about escaping reality
Everything goes the way you want it
Everything is great until the moment you open your eyes.
Reality is blinding, sleep is the antidote
Great waves of dismissal, I am indifferent
Make whatever comes my way jagged and piercing
For my dreams can wash me ashore.

I have a dream that I won't need dreams to excuse my reality
Because in the end, isn't that what living's all about?

The day I caught my first fish

Angelica Augustine

Aunty Erica is packing the tuckerbox for a day out fishing in one of our favourite fishing spots called Carnet Bay. The kids are running around with so much excitement that they're going to go swimming. The boys are getting the cars ready, they check the oil in both cars and fill up the radiators with water, they also load the food and slide their spear sticks through the windows of the cars.

'Jelly, get up, you coming fishing?' Aunty yells out from the kitchen. 'We're leaving soon, get up.'

'Yes, I'm coming,' I yell back with a tired but excited voice.

It's days like this I love most about living and growing up in the north-west of the Kimberleys. I get myself out of bed and change into my fishing clothes. I walk out to find the whole family packed and ready to go. The kids have their bathing suits on and some of us are sitting on the roof of the car with our towels above our heads blocking out the sun. The women and kids are taking the troopy and the boys are taking the Toyota. Sometimes the boys drive too fast so the kids are coming with us.

'Did you mob get the throw net?' Dad asks. 'We need to go before the tide comes in.'

'It's in the bucket,' we all call out.

We're all ready to go when Dylan says, 'Don't forget to pick up the dragnet from Nanna home for the coming-in tide and we need to get some ice from Grandpa home to put in the esky.'

Whenever we needed ice we knew just where to get it, Grandpa always has a freezer full of large blocks of ice. We drive to Nanna's place to pick up the dragnet while the boys are busting up ice on Grandpa's veranda. My grandmother and grandfather from my dad's side got married a long time ago, but live in separate houses almost next door to each other. We are about to leave when Gug* Ronny pulls up revving up the engine of his car. I jump in with him, Mum, and my little sister, Neemah. We're all going to the same place. We're all certain that we have everything and are ready to leave. When reversing out of Nanna's driveway she finally yells out, 'Bring me back fish.' We all respond with a yes and head out of Beagle Bay.

I love that feeling you get when you're travelling in the bush, hitting the humps and bumps, the wind blowing in your face so hard that the tears from your eyes start to run back to your ears. The freshness of the air reminds you that there's no place like home. The uncertainty of not knowing what we might come across on that red dirt road, maybe a huge, fat goanna, or turkey. We were always told to keep an eye out for them. Gug Ronny would always have his gun close by, it was a 22 Magnum rifle and he never missed. If we weren't doing that, my siblings and I would play this game where you had to find as many bird nests as you could before we stop at our destination. Whoever found the most nests won. I swear I had the best childhood ever growing up in the bush.

When we reach Carnet Bay the site is just breathtaking, the water is crystal clear. The sound of the birds singing peacefully in the trees while the whistling wind accompanies them, the waves crashing on the shore, bringing in beautiful seashells every time. Seagulls hunt for small baitfish in the shallows, rippling in schools of eighty. The boys jump out of the car as quick as they can and rush for their spears. They make their way to the mangroves hoping to catch a fat jinup* or a big mud crab for dinner. Everyone helps unload the car and set up camp while Dylan goes down the beach with a throw net to catch some bait. I follow behind with a bucket.

After setting up camp and taking the little ones for a swim I grab a handline from another bucket and tell Mum to fix it up for me, she puts on a size three sinker and a small hook. I cut a small piece of fish to use as bait and attempt to throw my line out. Gug Ronny says to try and get my hook and sinker under the dead hanging branches of the mangrove trees where there's a shadow, that's where all of the big red snappers and barramundi hang around he says. I listen. I hold my line out and swing it around on top of my head like a helicopter until I get the rhythm. I then let go and the sinker splashes exactly where I want it to land. Just a few seconds later, *bang*. Using fresh mullet for bait my line takes off.

'Play with him,' Gug Ronny says.

A tug-of-war takes place between me and the fish. I know it's not a barramundi because it doesn't jump out of the water, splashing trying to spit out my hook. This must be a big mangrove jack. The line burns my fingers, this fish has a lot of strength. I continue to play with him and slowly I can feel his strength starting to weaken. I give my one last pull as I'm walking up the beach and out of the water emerges a huge mangrove jack, the sun's reflection shimmers off his large red scales. Everyone is cheering and my uncle gives me that look, that look that says I'm proud of you my girl. Overwhelmed with excitement I give him a big hug.

**Gug/Uncle*
**Jinup/Saltwater Stingray*

Spearfishing

Danny Howard

the danger

the unknown deep

the quiet of the world beneath the ocean

dangerous and beautiful at the same time

Spear

Danny Howard

you
don't
pick
your
spear

your
spear
picks
you

Coast

Nancy Murray

A brilliant summer's day up the coast.

Fresh eyes scoped the entirety of the ocean. Home to one too many a beach memory. Nine-year-old me yearned for that salty tang of the sea breeze. I watched as my younger brother David clambered out of the car. We did most things together. Wearing colourful bathers, we raced to an empty shade-cloth area as Mum yelled, 'Quick! Before we lose it!' as a line of cars pulled up a distance away.[1] We anchored ourselves in cool sand and waited for Mum and Dad to come.

Fiddling with broken sticks, a crab scuttled past. A teeny one. Its home inches away from my feet. Curiosity got the best of me, I moved closer. David straightened up.

'Where're you goin'?'

'Nowhere!' I said.

I shuffled closer to the hole, hoping to hide the entrance from him. David had a thing for crawling things. Lizards, insects, little mice … if it had four or more legs, David found it like hens to grain.

---

[1] *a little bit of context*
One hour's drive from Carnarvon lay the Blowholes Sanctuary. The easiest way to escape whatever bullshit thing if you lived in the 'von. Bullshit for me at that time consisted of long days in a stuffy classroom in Yr. 4. I enjoyed doing schoolwork – Spelling, Maths, SOSE – but never much enjoyed Recess and Lunch.

The crashing of waves along the rocky coastline shifted my train of thought. Not far from where we were situated were the Blowholes: a mysterious spot where danger and beauty are one and the same. As if she had read my mind, Mum announces we're off for a walk over there. I always enjoyed the spectacle of it. The big *whooshing* of the water as it rushed up from below, as if some supernatural force was behind it. The build-up of sticky tension from the anticipation of something magnificent about to unfold, followed by the explosion of a million insignificant splashes. This was something that was witnessed from a distance.

As we made our way cautiously over to the cliff's edge, I sensed my brother's hesitance. His face was a mixture of stifled fear and pure excitement.

'Are we *reeeeally* gonna go right up?' David says.

'Yeah, we are.' I say back. 'Even better! Let's see who can stay right up at the edge for the longest!!'

Having known seven-year-old David, the opportunity was a given. The phrase *Wouldn't miss it for the world* in capital letters could've been a flashing neon sign on his forehead at that given moment. And we were off.

Rumbling from deep below, the feeling of promised unease filled us from the toes up. The feeling was similar to the monster underneath your bed – the unknown consuming you much more than the risk of physical harm. We both stood side by side like dolls in the shopfront, out for display ... The air shifted, and a niggling thought crossed my mind. As I looked down, there was no water.

I could see a teeny crab, wedged between two crevices. It was so similar to the one back on the beach.

I should've known better than to stand that close … It was too close.

To be continued …

I can do anything

Nancy Murray

When I look out from the window, I hope to see a better morning
  because I know waking up is sometimes the greatest thing in
  itself
Mornings are made for a fresh start, a clean slate clean from
  yesterday's layers of dirt
God-like, rise with the gods, euphoric even
Present wrapped in the sunrise, unravelled when the sun sets
  The sky is a myriad of colours that fills my daily cup.

All for new beginnings, no desire to continue with the old
Stretch and be new, red for wealth
Calm and unsettling, ease into chaos, home and lost, break even
Mind flowing, butter-like touch match the yellows in the sky
Orange Red Green followed by wicked Blues Violet Indigo …
Aren't we lucky?

Symphony upon symphony, harmoniously stacked
Only the finest musicians there playing melodies unimaginable
  – that's what waking up
  early in the morning feels like,
  you're on top of the world!
Crown caresses the sun as my curtain opens
The world at my feet

I can do anything.

the stuff of dreams

At two

Mabel Gibson

At two it's waking up to see your mother's eyes and making shapes from the clouds in the sky.

innocent, warm love.

At six it's getting butterflies when your crush chases you through the playground and you go to your Nan's house for dinner every Tuesday.

playful, fun love.

At twelve it's that knot in your stomach when he's holding hands with the pretty blonde girl and you turn to the boy from your favourite band who is plastered to your wall with blu tack.

hopeless, young love.

At fifteen it's you and him swinging and laughing in the park and summer nights spent swimming in oceans and losing your innocence.

beautiful, first love.

At seventeen it's the natural high you get from dancing and watching the neon lights illuminate his smiling face.

electric, glowing love.

The rainbow

Angelica Augustine

Why is black not in the rainbow?
Is it because it's too dark
and doesn't fit in with the brighter colours?

Just because it doesn't fit in
does that mean it shouldn't belong?
There's nothing wrong with being different.

I heard someone once say that black is the colour of death.
If so, what do the other colours represent?

I am

Mabel Gibson

I struggled with feeling like my life wasn't mine, I did not think it was my family's or friend's or anyone else's either. I'd stare at a body and a face and not be able to relate them to my thoughts or attach my name to them. My voice didn't sound like it belonged to me and when people called my name I had trouble understanding that it was mine. Sometimes I would imagine my soul floating around and it looked more like me than my skin and bones ever did. How do you show what kind of a person you are through your appearance? How do you wear your voice, your culture, your traumas and your greatest moments? How do you look like your soul, your heart and your thoughts? It took a long time for me to look in the mirror and think 'that is me'. I am glitter that won't leave my skin no matter how hard I try to wash it off. I am the blue finger that I have from wearing cheap rings. I am the shimmer in the generic shampoo that I use. I am the odd brown spot in my blue eyes. My soul reflects my appearance. I am beautiful in a curious way, I am unusual. That is me. Who I am and how I look, my thoughts, my face, my name, my body … they all reflect each other. They are all mine.

An Aboriginal woman with white skin

Connie Gamble

I grew up hating my skin
grew up wishing I looked like my cousins, beautiful, fierce and black.

My whole life people have questioned my identity and
Aboriginality.
'What percent are you?'
'You're too white to be Aboriginal'
'too nice to be Aboriginal'
'too pretty to be Aboriginal.'

'So you're a half-caste.'
'Who's black, Mum or Dad?'
'What percent is your dad?'
'Why don't you speak proper English?'
'Yeah but you're not one of them kind of Aboriginals.'

Growing up I knew my skin was white
but I always knew I was Aboriginal.
I was proud. Still am.
All I ever knew was my black family.

Me and my cousins were thick as thieves back in the day
where they was, I was.
We would always be at Nanna and Pop's
sitting on the porch
dancing and singing to old school RnB
thinking we was proper deadly.

As I've gotten older
I've realised my white skin isn't that bad.
I'm like a spy.

I see all the shit that my black sisters and brothers don't see.
I hear all the shit my black sisters and brothers don't hear.
People don't realise I'm black, so they let their ignorance slide.

I'm the one who sees both worlds.
I'm the one who hears both worlds.
I'm the one who stands up for my people.
I'm the one who understands my people.
I'm the one who feels their pain.

I shed tears for our people.
For all people of colour.
For all people who don't mould into the white society.

'I can't breathe.'
Every black person
when a brother or sister is killed by someone in a uniform.
Whether you're a black person
from America, Australia, Africa, New Zealand
and other places.
You hurt, we all hurt.

Why are we a threat?

Serena-May Brown

Why are we a threat when we reach for our phones?
Why are we seen as a threat to society?
Why are our lands being demolished and taken for money?
Why are we seen as a threat because of our colour?
Why are we seen as a threat when we breathe?
Why are we being killed for no reason?
Why has there been no change?
Why and when will this pain go away?

Stolen Generation

Jarrad Travers

If you didn't surpass
You got labelled half-caste
A stolen generation
From white man's impregnation

Their melanin just not prevalent
Yet its irrelevance evident
Training the black out
Leaves their lives in doubt

A spectrum of protrusion
Called for white man intrusion
A chemistry of supremacy
Helping them, allegedly

Christmas

Connie Gamble

My nana and pop lived in an old faded blue house on Paget Street, lined with jacaranda and flame trees. Everyone knew my nana and pop and loved them to bits. Every Christmas, my family would arrive from all over Australia to come to their house – the hub.

As a kid, I would jump straight out of the car and run up the old creaky stairs on to the porch and into the house, walking fast-paced past the lounge, the spare bedroom, through the hallway passing Nana's room, Raymond's room and past the bathroom straight into the kitchen, looking for Nana to give her a hug and kiss. Then I'd say hello to my family.

Nana's kitchen was somewhat small and really old with blue walls and at Christmas it would always be filled with decorations and the smell of something cooking. The house was never quiet – Pop yelling and arguing at the top of his lungs, my cousins and siblings running around, aunties telling us to behave, and Nana's favourite saying, 'Don't run in Nana's house.'

We'd carry trays of food out to the back veranda, preparing to feast on amazing home-cooked food. Aunties plated the kids' food first, then Nana's and Pop's, and after that anyone could grab their food and yarn around the table. There were all sorts of salads and meats – potato salad, pasta salad, green salad, potato bake, kangaroo, emu, beef and chicken – and all sorts of sweets.

Pop would stand and walk over to the Christmas presents that were underneath the tree out back. Nana would read the names out and Pop would give the presents to us. Presents weren't a big thing in my family and they were always small, but it didn't matter because we knew that money didn't buy happiness, love and family did.

Christmas today is different.

I don't see my cousins as often and most stay home. But for those who do come down, we head to the cemetery to see my uncle. Uncle Malcolm is my dad's oldest brother, he passed away when I was around twelve years old.

When we lost my uncle, it broke my family. We are still somewhat close but not as close as we were before. So, nowadays we spend Christmas at the cemetery blasting country music, reminiscing about the old days, just sitting with family, cleaning up Uncle Malcolm's and my cousin Jordan's headstones.

Rain, rain, never go away

Mabel Gibson

It may be raining outside, but when has that ever bothered you? You are the girl who loves the rain. You love how it styles your hair, and how your nose turns red. You never let how other people view the rain change how you feel about it. The colour of the sky doesn't make people sad, people make themselves sad. The rain makes you happy. Your childhood was Albany winters where the rain is nostalgic and the landscape is natural and stunning. You used to put on glittering bubblegum pink gumboots and dance in the sky's tears and collect hail to put in the freezer. Remember the child that you are, the one person who doesn't need an umbrella, the person who adores the feeling of rain on skin. You love to wear beanies and two pairs of socks. Think about how easy it is to sleep while the rain taps its fingers on your window and the wind sings to you. When your hands turn purple from the cold think about how purple is your favourite colour, a colour that has been with you longer than most of your friends. Feel the privilege of resembling something so loyal and true. Remember telling your doctor that you could marry June and that you spent days looking out the window hoping that summer never came. Forget about the people whose moods change with the weather, you are not that easily persuaded into being sad. Remember that you chose happiness. You chose happiness in the rain.

27 Jan 2017

Nancy Murray

Thoughts?

I think to myself
Why must life always
Revolve around others'
Beliefs and ideas, notions
And perceptions of you
You … You are everybody else's
Possession until
Ever-after.
Longing for the day
When I am no longer
The product of others' wishes
And something that I masterpieced
And thought of whilst dreaming.
Dreaming of better days,
Better days away from
My hometown, away
From anyone who saw me
So I then can recreate myself
Into the subject
of my own desire.

Light

Delivered into light
Honest and pure
Your parents grew you

Shaped you into their ideas of RIGHT from WRONG
Don't talk with your mouth full
Always say 'please' and 'thank you'
From age 5, unrelenting
Soaked, Washed, Rinsed and Repeat.

Darkness

Slumped
Drained of all life
I'm not my own and I know it
Taken of that circumstance
Which makes you hope for the
Stuff of happiness
Only realising that it
Will never be the case.

Opinions?

She feels like she is slowly dying. Just moving a hand or a finger seems draining. Draining ooouutt. Her very being seems on the verge of collapsing. Outside connections no longer conjure her spirit into redeeming itself. Words, words, mumbo jumbo. 'The pen is mightier than the sword' – but it takes time to strengthen the skills of the mind that utilises the pen. And vice versa for the sword. In saying so, it takes no genius to pick up a weapon and kill whoever wields the pen. The pen is useless and obsolete in terms of physical combat. Violence breeds more violence. Words, words thought out enough can bring out aspects of human nature that are more powerful than fear, anger, etc. Emotions such as hope, determination, forgiveness are main pillars in the pen's arsenal. It has these feelings in its favour.

Be mindful

'Wouldn't it be shit if somebody stopped doing something they were genuinely passionate about because another person laughed at them or told them that it was terrible ... saying the deed whilst unaware all the while destroying this person's inner metropolis.'

- Thoughts while self-reflecting

To be young and naïve is all I've ever ~~known~~ wanted

12.49 am 29/12/16

Paper rustling in the night.
Makes you wanna
Feel how the night caresses
The moonlit sea.
Ethereal
Momentum in the earth's pull
We float farther and farther
From the real Question;
Should I Stay?
(or Should I Go?)

Unoriginal

The same patterns repeat themselves
Intentionally, because we've all processed
The same information too many times, compare today
To yesteryear
The screen smiles
The childish antics play with my mind
Nobody knows
Except me

Understanding?

People come and go all the time. And although this is true, I believe that some of these people are meant to cross paths with you. Whether it be to teach you important lessons or add to your collection of loved ones.

Each individual, with an exception for newborn babies, have interesting and beautiful backstories. Quite often hidden from sight at first but with a little tweaking and light caressing, what is discovered is quite extraordinary.

Sweet nothings

Those honey words
How can I focus,
When the locusts gnaw my brain
How can I dream,
When the shouts and screams
Sing me awake!
How is there peace,
When all I think about is thinking
Loud ticking, 'round the circle
Reminding me
'You too will run out of time.'

Invite – refused

Come into my shell
Where treasures are hidden
Everything sits proud and upright
Nothing quivers to the sound of
That loud voice, deep in that dark valley

I speak with boldness and my words bulge with value
Nothing is alarming, for when I speak, the world stands still
I am now nature's master, her intention and mine now one and the same
So come in, I insist
To my refuge,
Where I am full and real
Come into my shell
And look at me
For I am no longer afraid

I want to live beautifully.
As in I want to find beauty in everything.

Fin.

Amy

Mabel Gibson

Amy is a girl. She has long black hair that hugs her hips. Her eyes are electric blue but sometimes when she wears green they can appear green; they are brightest and most noticeable when she has been crying. In winter her skin is pale, ice-like, and the tip of her nose is always red during those cold months.

Amy often looks out her window. She calls herself an observer and she would make a great scientist. Sometimes when she is looking out her window she sees Charlie ride past on his skateboard, he is tall and thin but she can see his eyes from her window on the second floor of her house. Already they have two things in common, their beautiful eyes and their love for skateboarding and they haven't even had a conversation yet.

Amy will watch Charlie for years. Eventually they will become best friends, they will spend all their time together and Amy will figure out that they have more in common than she has with anyone. She will fall in love. He will get a girlfriend and she will be tall like him, she will have blonde hair and she will be tanned all year round.

Amy will not help but notice that her eyes are a grey, dull colour. He will spend less time with Amy and more with her, until they break up.

Amy will counsel him through the break up. He will date other people, and so will she. In her heart there is always a place for him and some nights she hopes that he will turn around and confess that he has loved her all these years too. When they are older he will meet a girl and they will get married.

Amy will attend the wedding and try to smile.

Amy will settle and eventually get married too and have children, but late at night Amy will think about how things might be if she had told Charlie that she loved him.

Stolen

Jarrad Travers

(published in *Australian Poetry Journal 7.1* 'SKIN' coedited by Ellen van Neerven and Ali Cobby Eckermann)

I'm sorry, I'm sorry
It was never enough.
Our ancestors and grandparents they're oh so tough.
But years ago
Were taken away.
By that white man.
Led my grandfather astray. How did they live?
In a world so grey.
Surviving not thriving
On a mission for change.
But why was that
A necessity for them?
Was it so
I did not condemn?
But why? I still ask.
They were morally bankrupted. I now live my life
Sorrily, disgusted.

What do you do?

Mabel Gibson

What do you do when your friend comes to you and says, 'I slept with a boy last night and now I feel sick'? What do you do when you know that she couldn't possibly have consented to sleeping with him because she was drunk? What do you do when she's laughing but she doesn't actually find it funny? How do you tell her that you think she has been sexually assaulted? How do you tell her when you think deep inside she already knows this herself? I know very well that after sex you should not feel disgusted in yourself, you shouldn't spend the day with your head in the sink throwing up and when you see the guy next, whether it be a day later or a year later, you shouldn't have an anxiety attack. Sex. I am not afraid to say that sex is freedom, sex is liberating and when my friends tell me about their sexual experiences I don't think 'slut', I don't think 'whore', I am a 21st-century girl and I believe in sexual freedom. I start to worry though when my friend comes to me and she's laughing but she's also crying because last night she got drunk and she went to a boy's room to watch Stan and the next thing she knows they are having sex and when they are finished she doesn't feel pleasured or freed, she feels sick and ashamed. She never said no but she never said yes. What does she do now? She laughs about it, she says, 'Guess who I slept with last night ... you're going to think it's so funny.' And I do, I think it's funny until I realise she was drunk and he was sober. I think it's funny until I realise that her eyes aren't showing the same emotion that her laugh is. I think it's funny until she says when she woke up the morning afterwards she felt guilty and sick. I laughed with her until I didn't think it was funny, I thought it was rape.

I don't feel like dying today

Mabel Gibson

I don't feel like dying today because I want my ten-year-old sister to
have a normal life.
I don't feel like dying today because I don't want to break my parents'
hearts.
I don't feel like dying today because I've been waiting for winter all
summer.
I don't feel like dying today because my dog won't understand.
I don't feel like dying today because there are so many interesting
people I haven't met.
I don't feel like dying today because I haven't finished reading *Harry
Potter and the Cursed Child.*

I don't feel like dying today because I want to see my sister become a
nurse.
I don't feel like dying today because I don't know who would look
after my chilli plant.
I don't feel like dying today because my grandparents have lost too
many people already.
I don't feel like dying today because I haven't been to France yet.
I don't feel like dying today because I want to get to know him better.
I don't feel like dying today because my friends already have enough
on their plates as it is.
I don't feel like dying today because The 1975 is coming to Perth in
September.
I don't feel like dying today because I want to watch my brother shine.
I don't feel like dying today because my skin is starting to look better.
I don't feel like dying today because I haven't finished living yet.

Foreign

Nancy Murray

Too long, we remain silent,
Too long, it's just about their rules.
Foreign. Defined as 200 or so years.
You call us many names. Native. Aboriginal. Indigenous. But we have many names ourselves. We are too distinct to carry one name.
We are as many as there are grains of sand and distinct as there are fingerprints on your hand.
What kind of right do you have,
To uproot this land's peoples, to seek unjust claim and to declare yourselves
Rulers of this richness to hunger over for just yourselves

What kind of rules do you have?
We have rules that have been here before anything else.
Over-arching utopia, for generations
Lore was constant, lore was meaningful
And it still is.
The land and us are intermeshed.
What do you have to bring to the table?
Systemic violence guised as government's agenda.
A government not meant for us.

Time's changing, Today's a time our ancestors,
Would have never dreamt of for us.
Today, there's hope.
Light carried on from our strong nans and pops.
Our resilient ancestors, our Elders.

We have a means to an end.
Finally, are we able to make our own destiny?
In this Other world, can we finally better
The futures of our sons and daughters?
Determine our lives,
Make it the fruits of our own thoughts.
May we eat and thrive all together?
At this new table, we might feast and laugh …
Together.

Stand still ...

Connie Gamble

(published in *Australian Poetry Journal 7.1* 'SKIN' coedited by Ellen van Neerven and Ali Cobby Eckermann)

It's the 21st century
but why does it feel like the 20th century?
Lives taken,
children never feelin' safe,
curled up inside skin
they've been taught to hate.
The rattling of chains from our recent history,
'just get over it, it was in the past.'
Now how can you put something in the past
when it hasn't stopped,
when children are still taken away
and culture is still being lost.

Me

Brianne Yarran

He painted me
And now everyone sees
But they don't see
The real Lisa, me
I cry behind the glass
In hope that this will never last
Praying for the day
They will all stay away
I haven't been alone
Never had the chance to touch a phone
Yet I see 3 million a year
And with each visitor I shed a tear
The world has evolved and changed
As I stay the same but others are rearranged
I hear kind words from loving hearts
But some words have felt like darts
I see my reflection every day
And I see the paint is slowing wearing away
I was happy and loved
But now this is not enough
Yes, I am gone, yes I am dead
But my spirit lives on through my eyes and head
It is always loud in here
And yet my voice was never clear
A painting can tell a thousand words
And yet I am silenced never to be heard.

Unseen

Mabel Gibson

i had no chance as soon as he saw me. i could see thoughts on his face like the freckles were turning into words, 'oh, she doesn't look like her pictures.' But neither did he. He said 'you're just such a great personality, most girls can't hold a conversation like you' but i don't care what most girls do because although he liked my personality i knew he thought that the package was ugly. i knew that he was expecting it to be wrapped in shiny pink wrapping paper not grey newspapers. This isn't the first time i figured that looks count and it won't be my last. i worked myself up for days and days, and in the morning i threw up in my sink and on the bus i was so anxious i cried. i knew i wasn't someone he would stop on the street for, but i wouldn't stop for him either. When we sat down he talked to me about his family as if he wanted to introduce me to them, right then and there. 'I'll see you again soon.'

i knew when he saw me he'd be disappointed, so why did i go? Maybe when i looked at his profile a part of my brain thought 'well i may not be a model, but so nor is he.' In the end it came down to looks. Maybe i'm bigger than he expected, maybe i dress like a homeless person and maybe i look like i haven't slept since 2015. He chose a girl with a flat stomach instead of my ability to make him laugh. He chose a girl who does her hair every day instead of the girl who shares all his favourite movies. And he chose a girl with a pretty face instead of, well, me. And he said 'sorry for wasting your time' and i thought 'no, i'm sorry for wasting yours' because i know that i'm not the pretty girl. i knew it for days before and i knew it when my head was over my bathroom sink and i knew it when i cried on the bus on the way home.

Zenaida

Angelica Augustine

She's beautiful, so small and innocent / Her face, smooth and chubby / Her eyes, oh her eyes
They are brighter than the brightest light / Like a lamp in the centre of a dark room
She is special in every way / She is God's masterpiece / Handcrafted by him, and for him
She has her mother's nose / And the eyes of her father / She is the female version of her brother

You don't know me yet, but you will very soon
Because you are growing up so fast
I will always be here for you,
When you laugh
But mostly when you cry
I love you my little angel.

Dream like a child

Mabel Gibson

Childish. What is so wrong with being childish? Childhood is the closest reality we have to magic. Why can't I have my head in the clouds but still have my feet on the ground? I want to dream like a child. I want to believe that beautiful fairies in purple tutus live within the trees. I want to lay on the grass and see the clouds make the shape of a dragon. I want to believe that the first star to appear at night is my dead uncle, glittering in the sky to tell me he is here. I want colour in my mind and all over my body. I want to leave a trail of glitter when I walk. I want to lay on the carpet next to my window and drown in the sunshine. I want people to know that within all these things there is magic. If you can dream, you can feel magic. If you can swim in the ocean, you can feel magic. To be five and have your face light up when you see your dad, that is magic. To be thirteen and see your favourite band live, to be seventeen and walk under the stars with your best friend. To think that the sky is crying when it rains, to fly through galaxies and still be able to work from 9 to 5. It is all real magic. Magic is not a child's game, magic is real.

sunrises are my eyes

Unravel the unravel-able

Nancy Murray

Remember times when you were little when you'd be full of energy sleeping in the same bed as your parent/grandparent wanting to talk to them but they were not awake and you'd think sitting watching them because they are your world and you are at their feet because without them you would not even exist and you love them with all your heart but you don't say it much because you think that life is uninterrupted and time will wait for you and you'll have the chance to but truth be told life is ruthless and unkind.

But it doesn't wait … and then you're feeling sick and stuck in the thought of someday Disappearing

Blithering on about the mundane every day.
Cherish everything because everything is everything
Hang onto it, suck it dry
That juicy, dripping beauty in the world
The way someone looks when they smile and they mean it
The way the morning sun gets into every nook with its beam
I dance in days like this.

Unpack lovely, lovely words
Speak only these kinds of words
You know with a look
And not what you say
Nothing needs translation or paraphrasing
Raw and real, I understand I'm wasting my time
With trying to unravel the unravel-able.

7.23 in the morning

Angelica Augustine

Here I am again.
I am woken by the sound of birds
singing peacefully in the trees.
The whistling wind accompanies them.

Waves crash on the shore
bringing pretty seashells with them.
Seagulls hunt for small bait in the shallows
rippling in schools of eighty.

I lie in bed thinking about my life and the decisions I have to make.
An eighteen-year-old girl who just graduated high school.
I can feel the stresses of life coming down on me.

He's not worth your time

Mabel Gibson

'He's not worth your time.' It's not really like that though, is it? It's not that he's not worth my time, it's that I'm not worth his. If he doesn't give you time, or barely acknowledges you then he clearly thinks you are not worth his time. So why do they say the opposite? Why tell me that he's not worth my time when he is, because I would give him the time and I would do it happily. He *is* worth my time. How do you become worth something as complex as time? And how could I happily spend the rest of time, every second, every beam of sunlight and every drop of rain with him? That question becomes even more impossible to answer when he can't even think of time to spend on me. I don't think it's ever a two-way street when it comes to how a person values their time, it's always a one-way street and only one person can ever drive on it at a time. It feels good though, you can change your whole life when you realise the things that are meant to be and those things that aren't. Lately I am learning to love the sound of my feet walking away from things not meant for me. And when you realise that you aren't worth a person's time you begin to wonder what you are doing, who you are, and why others are worth your time? And when I thought hard enough about this I walked away, I didn't say goodbye, I didn't say anything, I just walked away. It wasn't hard either, it was the easiest thing I ever did. And now he's not worth my time, regardless if I'm still not worth his or even if I am. My time is my own.

Love

Mabel Gibson

I once read somewhere that most people fall out of love for the same reasons they fell in it. When people used to ask me what I fear most in life I would say things like car crashes or grown adults dressed as animals. When people ask my greatest fear now how do I tell them the thing that keeps me up at night is the fact that a lover's once edgy stubbornness has now become a refusal to compromise and their one-track mind is now childish. Their bad habits that once gave them a rebellious edge are now money down the drain. Their spontaneity becomes reckless and irresponsible. But how do I also tell them that the thought of someone falling out of love with me for the same reasons they fell in love with me is my greatest fear. There is nothing on Earth that scares me more than the thought that someone who once saw me as a beautiful glittering star could see me as ugly and just another part of their busy life.

Home town

Savannah Cox

I walk out onto the balcony with a cold glass of fresh milk and a silver spoon that has just been dipped into a jar of Nutella. I sit on the blue and white striped hammock that hangs out on my balcony in a position I would say is perfect for many reasons. During the day it sits in the shade where I can lay my feet and feel the coastal breeze flow through my body. At night I can look up and gaze at the stars and wait for the moon to rise as it turns from orange-red to grey-white. I look west towards the coast and see the sun peeking behind the tall palm trees and two-storey houses.

I glance at the clock through the window, 5.10 pm. 'We still have time to go if we leave now, Khan,' I shout through the flyscreen door.

He sits himself up while turning off the TV and darts into the room. I walk into the house to place my spoon in the sink and chug down the rest of my milk. I grab my keys on the way out as Khan follows behind pulling on a white T-shirt. 'If I stay in this house any longer I will go crazy,' he says while nearly slipping on the way down the stairs. We both laugh for a few minutes. We jump into the little silver Hyundai and zoom off onto the highway.

'What the hell is happening here?' I say looking around at the filled parking lot. I turn down a lane and manage to find a spot not too far from the entrance. We both jump out and make our way up the hill. The smell of fresh fish and chips being cooked fills the air as we reach the top. People are scattered everywhere across the beach. The majority are lazing around on towels and camping chairs, having a beer or just enjoying the view.

Khan and I make our way down the flight of stairs in single file as people walk up and down. I take off my shoes and feel the smooth, soft sand under my feet.

'You find us a spot and I'll go get us some food,' Khan says. He gives me a peck on the lips before walking back up.

I look around and see a spot just below the sand dunes and I walk over to inspect the area. I sit down and start to play with the sand, letting it slip through my fingers and down to my legs. Repeating it over and over while waiting patiently for Khan to return with food. A calm breeze blows through the air with various shapes of clouds filling the colourful sky. Boats sail on the ocean blackened from the descending sun replicating a silhouette painting.

Khan appears and sits, placing the white foam container in front of us. I kiss him on the cheek and thank him as we start to eat the hot fish and chips with tartar sauce. While we eat I take a moment to look around me.

'I am damn lucky,' I think to myself. I'm in my beautiful home town of Broome, stress-free, doing what I love with the person I adore most in this world. No worries or burdens.

Yeah, that's right, I am damn lucky.

Sugar

Nancy Murray

Sugar in my hair, melting everywhere
The rush gives me the fix, I love the taste
It oozes on my tongue and smooths out all that bitterness
From the hard-knock life, from the hard-knock lies
Just gimme that hit and I'll be mostly fine.

Lick that stick of gum and chomp on that gobstopper
Pain equals pleasure, not many people can dig that
More of a miracle that we find delight in the simpler things
Bang! Zap! Pow!
No, I love the taste.

Enormous words come from tiny mouths
The zestiness of this lollipop makes me salivate
And beg for more, the icing covers the cake
Bright, artificial flavouring – sings on my palate
One
More
Bite

The feeling's indescribable.
The feeling you can only get when you sink your
Teeth into a warm
Freshly
Baked
Cookie

Just the way I like it.

Doubt

Nancy Murray

Doubt
Caresses my scalp
Nibbles at my tissue
Gnaws and compresses
… I feel fine.

Like a crown he sits
Nestled soundly
Waiting and watching
For those fleeting moments when
I least expect it.

Umming and ahhing
Latched on this heavy weight
A groaning burden
He quietly mumbles
You're not worth it.

Never in your best days
Are you worth it.

Van Gough

Mabel Gibson

Vincent Van Gough ate yellow paint because it was a happy colour and he believed if he ate it the happiness would be inside him. I saw this post when I was thirteen and along with thousands of other people from all over the world who had liked, commented and shared the post I wondered what my yellow paint would be. It wasn't until I became extremely passionate about Van Gough and his work did I realise that he did not eat yellow paint to be happy, he ate yellow paint as an attempt to poison himself and die.

Vincent Van Gough was riddled with mental illness. Throughout his life he stayed at several 'insane asylums' and was later labelled with many mental disorders including: paralysing anxiety, acute mania with generalised delirium, borderline personality disorder, chronic depression and bipolar disorder. Vincent Van Gough was sick. Vincent Van Gough tried to kill himself by eating paint and now it is being romanticised. I have seen fourteen-year-old girls post on their Tumblr blogs telling their followers to *find their yellow paint,* using Van Gough's suicide attempt as an inspiring fight for happiness. People are telling the story of something as morbid as death and making it sound as beautiful as happiness. Van Gough's life was not beautiful, his life was full of psychotic experience, one night he even cut off his left ear and handed it to a woman named Rachel. The next morning he didn't remember doing it.

Van Gough's life of mental illness has either frightened or inspired, neither of these emotions should be a reaction to Van Gough's life. He was just a man who was very sick, nothing inspiring and nothing frightening about it. There is a difference between normalising and romanticising and this difference should be considered when we discuss mental illness. It is normal for a patient diagnosed with psychosis to not sleep, but it is not beautiful. The bags under their eyes look heavy not aesthetic and their dissociative nature is not beautiful, they are tired. It is normal for a person diagnosed with clinical depression to not want to get out of bed for a week, but a person who has not showered for a week is not beautiful. It is not beautiful to be scared of stepping outside of your house or to wake up every day and not be able to eat because you are so anxious, but that doesn't mean that these things are not normal for people experiencing mental illness. Normal does not have to be beautiful, we can get used to the ugly, horrific tragedies of life without fearing it.

Mental illness has jumped from one end of the spectrum to the other. Twenty years ago humans were horrified of mental illness and these days every second person is 'depressed', and your ex-boyfriend is a 'psychopath', and the girl in your class who got angry once, well she had 'bipolar'. When I was in high school I was hospitalised for two weeks because I was dead inside and that is truly the only way to describe it. When I went back to school after those two weeks a group of my friends asked me what happened. I have never been afraid of speaking about mental illness so I told them. For the rest of lunch I had to listen to seven girls argue about who is more depressed. They were literally fighting to be the most unhealthy person in the circle. They, along with so many other people today, viewed depression as beautiful.

If my friends think mental illness is beautiful they sure didn't see me for those two weeks. I was paler than the codeine that I had to take every three hours because depression equals physical pain. The amount of oil in my hair could have been used to deep fry a whole chicken because I was too weak and too numb to get out of bed and wash my hair and I still have scars on my face from those two weeks because I spent most of my time picking at my skin. Those two weeks were the ugliest of my life and I had seven girls telling me that I was lucky that the doctors hospitalised me and that they wished their parents would take them to hospital.

I beg for the people who claim that Van Gough's life was a beautiful tragedy to stop. I have heard people discuss Van Gough's life and make remarks such as, *If people had just bought his work while he was alive he might have wanted to live a little longer.* But I would argue that considering his mental state I do not think that he would have. I do not think that a man going in and out of insane asylums, being described with several mental illnesses would care if his work was recognised or not. If someone were to have bought a piece of Van Gough's work I doubt very much that Van Gough would remember it had been bought by the next morning. I would argue that he was too sick to mind at all.

It is normal to be sick. Having a mental illness is normal, it is not beautiful. Suicide is not beautiful, suicide just makes you dead. Suicide is how Van Gough became dead. Insomnia is not beautiful, insomnia puts the mind in a dissociative state. Depression is not beautiful, depression makes it hard to function as a human being. Mental illness is not beautiful, but it is normal.

My uncle could draw

Mabel Gibson

A man at a bank who I hardly knew.
A man that had so much left to do.
A thin white guy whose name was Paul,
A guy who I loved most of all.
When I look at my brother, Paul's who I see.
But he's not who I want my brother to be.

My uncle could draw.
Two coloured-in men walking toward a building
are held on my wall with blu tack.
I look at them at night when I wish Paul would come back,
'Life is not what it seems,' he tells me,
When he haunts me in my dreams.
and I say back, 'I know that, thanks to you.'

Paul was educated.
A man with talent.
A handsome guy
Who was living a lie.
He's not what he seemed.

He taught me about life
by not living anymore.
When I was young he used to call.

He took his money.
He used it all.

A heroin high, his last goodbye.
But oh god, my uncle could draw.

Glennup rubbish tip

Nancy Murray

The Glennup rubbish tip. I come here often. I arrive in my sun-bleached Toyota Camry every Sunday at noon to see if anything new has made the tip its home. I've recovered many treasures here, last-minute gifts for whatever the occasion. Birthdays, Valentine's, Christmases, the lot.

There's a whole process to digging up these things. I've gotta be wearing my lucky shoes, socks, hat. I have to be wearing every colour of the day otherwise I don't go out there. Today, I've chosen to start on the eastern side. That's where I think the nuggets are. I find the usual useless riff-raff. Broken tennis racquets, chipped television sockets and brand-new washing machines that worked and then they didn't.

I spot the skeleton of a once magnificent jukebox. Towering over a dead deciduous lies more rubbish. I get that special feeling. I begin to dig and dig and dig and dig. Nothing beats the strung-out process of it. The smell of dirt mixed with other substances, layers upon layers of history. Those that came before left behind parts of themselves, not knowing themselves. Dented bicycle spokes, abandoned baby clothes … again I've seen them all.

The hole widens and I start to lose hope. But the shovel says otherwise as it makes contact with something with a loud *crack* …

I sift the powdery dirt aside and pull out what looks like a piece of old china from underground. Another success in the life of a garbage grave-digger!

The lucky country

Savannah Cox

Australia, the mighty down under.
The country where it is constantly summer.
The beaches are beautiful and the scenery is great,
every person is either a 'sheila' or a 'mate'.

From the rugged Snowy Mountains,
to the sacred Uluru,
to the green rainforests of Queensland,
you are bound to see a roo.

This country is indeed
a must-see destination,
people travel the globe
to see this young and free nation.

'We've golden soil and wealth for toil'
All this wealth is from digging up gas and oil.
Destroying everything that sits upon the land,
anything for economic demand.

This county may have
beauty of rich and rare soil,
but is owned by foreign countries.
This makes my blood boil.

Australian land does not belong to anyone
other than the Indigenous people of this nation

yet the government is ignorant and worries more
about gender equality discrimination.

These foreign countries come here,
and destroy the land,
then pay us back with money, royalties,
and expect us to shake hands.

This country isn't all what it seems to be,
this is a land that is neither young nor free.
Come and have a look at the life we Indigenous people have to live daily.
You will go away frustrated and even slightly angry, maybe?

The signs

Serena-May Brown

It can be hard mapping your future
You have a journey you'd like to travel
To reach your aspirations
But the direction sometimes feels unsure

My heart says I should be there now
But my mind stops me
And reminds me
I'm doing something that will get me there
Eventually

I open my eyes
And let this frustration go

I will find my future
I see it
The structure
In my mind
A vision of what is mine

Australia's future is bright

Brianne Yarran

full of unity and truth
as we hear the voice of the youth
elders say education is key
all it takes is for me to believe

believe in justice and in healing
then we can go back to the time of dreaming
so close your eyes and think of a time
a time of equality between you and I

Dream

Brianne Yarran

Our people, our land, our rights
We have always put up the fights
Fights for our voice
When we didn't have a choice

'67 counted us
but still we have no trust
they took our children away
yet the pain remains every day

the Whadjella refused culture
but this just created vultures
angry children with no home
making them feel like nothing and alone

but when they looked up above
they dreamt of something called love
love that now begins to exist
as we say 'black power' with our fist

the constitution will change
and a treaty will be arranged
the voice of the future is near
as all in Parliament say 'hear hear'

there is agreement from all
as we stand proud and tall
black or white

I wish I were a fairy

Nancy Murray

I wish I were a fairy, wafting through air
No one to tell me right from wrong, my wings and I are one
Pixie dust, lalaland, everything sweet nothing sour
I wish that I could rise and set like the sun
According to the clock lodged deep within my body
Tick tock, tick tock, tick
… and not the Man's

Many times I imagine myself outside my own body
Within the reaches of pure emotion, pure thought
When times get rough, I look into then out of
Myself, eyes wrapped in cloth
Light a match, gasoline and
Light that match, ignite

Escaping into the made-up makes me content
To be alive, to experience things
My dreams are collages of what was seen
And what wasn't … seen

When will I realise, that life is ever-changing
When will I realise, you get what you grant to others
When will I realise, that no thing is ever given without hardship
When is now and now means forever

An eternity of nows
… Forever and ever

Mind palaces

Nancy Murray

My mind is not a playground
I barely like to acknowledge its existence
let alone swing on the monkey bars.
It's a work in progress though
there is too much room for failure
and failing is not a risk I'm willing to take.
Ever notice how beautiful you are, when your mind is floating
  feather-like?
No concern for others, only yourself
yet you worry so much about the thoughts of others
the normal persuasion …
Your blame reaches physicality, femininity, masculinity.
We can't all be your mothers.
Ever wonder how your mind plays tricks when you feel like nobody
  is watching but there is
someone watching?
Our own palaces need catering to
before we have
the sun in the sky
and the shimmer
of the stars at night
to care for
yours.

Contributors

Angelica Augustine is a Nyul Nyul woman from the Beagle Bay community in the Kimberley. In her spare time, she loves to go out fishing and camping with her family. Angelica has always had a passion for writing and feels privileged to have her work published by Magabala Books, alongside some of her good friends.

Serena-May Brown is a Torres Strait Islander woman from Moa Island, which has strong connections to Darnley Island and Badu Island. She was born in Perth and grew up in Karratha, a town of the Pilbara region of Western Australia. She is at the University of Western Australia studying a Bachelor of Arts majoring in Media and Communications and enjoys photography, playing guitar, painting and writing poetry. She is passionate about storytelling and plans on making her own films and plays in the future.

Savannah Cox is a young Yawuru, Karrajarri and Nimanburr woman who is from the town of Broome in the Kimberley region of Western Australia. She is currently a student at the University of Western Australia with a goal of completing a Bachelor of Arts, majoring in Indigenous Knowledge, History and Heritage.

Constance (Connie) Gamble is a Yamaji Naagufa Kiwi Woman. Her family is from Meekatharra, Western Australia, and her mother is from Oamaru on the South Island of New Zealand. Connie grew up in Fremantle. She has a passion for culture, family, friends and learning.

Mabel Gibson is a Yamatji woman studying Arts at the University of Western Australia. Her childhood was spent in Albany before moving to Geraldton as a teenager. Mabel's work has been published in *Once: A selection of short short fiction*, Night Parrot Press, 2020.

Danny Howard is a part of many places across Western Australia; these include the Barrd, Nunda, Yamaji, Noongar and Bunuba nations. He has lived on Baniol Barrd Country for most of his life, the Country where his grandfather (father's side) is from. He chose to write his two pieces, 'Spearfishing' and 'Spear', because they are both important Cultural practices that he carries out and celebrates when at home. Being a saltwater man, he loves the sea and the tucker that it supplies and these two pieces mean a lot to him. Danny is happy that he got the chance to share his Culture and knowledge with other aspiring minds.

Nancy Murray is a Barkindji woman from the far west riverland regions of NSW, but has lived on Yamatji country in the north-west tropical town of Carnarvon for the majority of her life. She is currently studying a Bachelor of Science, majoring in Conservation Biology and Indigenous Knowledge, History and Heritage. She is particularly keen on the arts, and is usually listening to music or watching films in her down-time.

Jarrad Travers is a Yamatji, Nyikina and Bardi teenager who was born in the remote town of Derby in the Kimberley region of Western

Australia. He is a student at UWA studying Law and Society and enjoys travelling, spending time with friends and writing poetry.

Brianne Yarran is a proud Whadjuk, Balladong and Wagyl Kaip Noongar woman from the South West of Western Australia. She is currently in her third year studying a Bachelor of Arts at the University of Western Australia, completing a double major in Law and Society and Indigenous Knowledge, Heritage and History. Brianne is passionate about Indigenous education at all levels.

Editors

Elfie Shiosaki is a Noongar and Yawuru writer. She is a lecturer in Indigenous Rights at the School of Indigenous Studies at the University of Western Australia and Editor of Indigenous Writing at *Westerly*.

Linda Martin is a lecturer in creative writing at the School of Indigenous Studies at the University of Western Australia. She is a professional editor and is co-publisher at Night Parrot Press.

Illustrator

Kamsani Bin Salleh is descended from the Nimunburr and Yawuru people of the Kimberley and the Ballardong Noongar people of the Perth region in Western Australia. His intricate designs are inspired by the natural world.

Also from Magabala Books ...

JULIE JANSON

BENEVOLENCE

GUWAYU–
FOR ALL TIMES
A COLLECTION OF
FIRST NATIONS POEMS
Commissioned by
Red Room Poetry
Edited by
Jeanine Leane

KINDRED
KIRLI SAUNDERS

LIVING ON
STOLEN LAND
Ambelin Kwaymullina

ature
can
swirl
like
a
alling
eaf
ruby moonlight
ali cobby eckermann
Winner of the Windham-Campbell Prize

GUS HENDERSON

THE WOUNDED SINNER

Us
Women,
Our
Ways,
Our
World
Edited by Pat Dudgeon, Jeannie Herbert,
Jill Milroy and Darlene Oxenham